Arthur

Book #4 in the TIME SOLDIERS® Series

By KATHLEEN DUEY

Created & Photographed by
ROBERT GOULD

3D Special Effects & Digital Illustration by
EUGENE EPSTEIN

The adventures

Six neighborhood kids discover something strange in the woods. They can't convince their parents that it exists. But it's real. Through a swirling portal of green-golden light, they see a live dinosaur! They pack their camping gear and go through, armed with a video camera. They brave many dangers but return safely.

The portal opens again the very next day; then nearly a year goes by before it opens a third time. The adventures are amazing—dinosaurs, pirates, and time travel!

continue...

But there are mysteries: They can't figure out when or why the time portal opens. Jon suffered a weird, terrible headache coming back last time. The pirates had a strange glowing jewel. No matter how long it seems like they've been gone, only an hour has passed at home. Strangest of all, mysterious men in dark suits stole their videotape.

The Time Soldiers are waiting. They're as prepared as they can be — they've studied history, survival skills and kept their gear ready. And now, finally, the portal is opening once more... .

"If I get a headache like last time," Jon said as they walked, "you guys go on without me."

Everyone nodded. Jon moved forward into the light and at first, he was all right. As always, there were misty shapes beyond the portal. He couldn't tell what they were. Then, without warning, the pain exploded inside his head.

It was so bad that he fell to his knees. A second later, Mariah stumbled and screamed. Then Adam doubled over.

"Turn back!" Rob shouted. "Turn back!"

Mariah and Adam leaned on each other as they staggered out of the portal. Jon barely made it out. The pain was terrible.

The men in dark suits were frowning. "Look at that," one of them said. "Three! All at once! Maybe these aren't the Originals. I thought—"

"You mean you *hoped*," his companion interrupted. "We have no choice now but to interfere and—"

"No!" The first man cut him off. "Let's see how they deal with it. Switch to the clubhouse cams."

Bernardo stared out at the trees. None of this made sense.

Jon was still talking. "It goes away, but…. Mariah couldn't even get out of bed. Adam? Are you OK?"

Adam grimaced. "My head still hurts. It was pretty bad last night."

Rob took a deep breath. "With only three of us, traveling will be too dangerous."

"Jon saved us all last time," Bernardo reminded them. "You three are the strongest, the oldest…." He looked up. "Is that it? You're too old, like in Peter Pan or something?"

No one laughed.

Mikey thought about it. "If that's it, we have to find replacements."

The men in dark suits stared at the holograms. "I think they have settled on these two," one said. "The girl's name is Caitlin—she's Mariah's cousin. The boy is Brian. They all trust him. Both of them seem smart and capable."

His companion nodded. "Then we still have a chance at the—"

"Shhh!" the other man hissed. "I want to hear what they're saying." He touched the screen. The room filled with children's voices. Jon was explaining the time portal to the two newcomers. Then he told them they would have to study and train hard to be Time Soldiers.

The first real meeting was on a hot, sunny day. It was cool and quiet in the library—a place the Time Soldiers all loved. Mariah assigned different subjects and split up the study load. At noon, they took a break.

"When will it open again?" Caitlin asked.

Rob shrugged. "There's no way to know."

Brian stood up and stretched. "Then we should start training tomorrow."

Bernardo sighed. "You have no idea how tough Jon and Adam can be on the rest of us."

Every morning for the next month, they ran in the woods. They spent days in the library, studying world history, looking up dozens of old-fashioned skills. Rob practiced archery. Brian took riding lessons. Mikey worked on making fire. Caitlin memorized maps. They all climbed ropes and ran agility courses. They all learned Morse code.

"What should we take?" Caitlin asked, looking at their survival gear. "Heavy coats? Sandals?"

"Depends. Where are you planning to go?" Mariah teased her. "Alaska in 1940 or Tahiti in 5000 BC?"

They all laughed.

Finally, after a month of waiting, they spotted the swirling light in the woods. They ran to the clubhouse to get their gear. As they hurried back, Mikey turned to Adam. "I wish you guys could come."

Adam shook his head. "Me, too. But that headache was unbelievable."

He raised his voice so they could all hear. "The new digital camera and the two-way radios are working perfectly."

"Caitlin, Brian…remember," Jon added as they walked, "it's sort of like being a family. You take care of each other."

"See you in an hour!" Adam called. "Be careful!"

Brian and Caitlin walked into the light. It swirled around them like a river current. The others followed.

"Stay hidden!" Rob cautioned once they were on the other side.

Caitlin's heart was pounding. "We're in ancient England!"

Bernardo looked around. "Or France, maybe?"

Brian pointed at two strangely dressed people.
"That boy is wearing a flaxen tabard. The design
is Roman influenced," Caitlin said. "And those
dark green trees along the creek are yews. I'd say
England, between 600 and 1100 AD, midsummer
from the looks of the berry bushes." She glanced

up at the sky. "About six in the evening? Five?"
Rob stared in disbelief. Mikey shook his head.
"She's Mariah's cousin," Bernardo reminded them.
"Shhh!" Brian warned. "They'll hear us."

The men in dark suits had been arguing.
"At least the helmet-cameras are working well.
Try switching through the whole sequence,"
one said.
The screens flashed.
"Good." The other man leaned forward.
"Middle Ages? That looks like Merlin."

The first man looked up sharply. "Stop joking."
The second man smiled. "Do you have a better explanation?"

"There has to be one," said the other. "King Arthur is a legend, a fairy tale."

"You must find the sword, Arthur," the old man said as he and the boy got closer. "Go to the mountain village and pull it from the stone. Prove that you are the one true king."

"I will," the boy promised, "but come with me, Merlin."

The old man smiled. "This is *your* task, young Arthur. You will find the courage to overcome the dangers. And you will have plentiful help if you need it."

The Time Soldiers ducked lower as the old man turned to peer through the bushes. Brian's eyes met Merlin's for an instant.

"He saw us," Brian breathed. "He looked right at me."

"This is too weird," Caitlin whispered back. "Merlin and Arthur? That's not history. It's a legend!"

Rob was frowning. "*King* Arthur?" He got the digital camera out of his pack. "The one who pulled a sword out of solid rock?"

Bernardo nodded. "Who else could it be?"

Brian looked thoughtful. "In the story, a lot of people tried to keep him from becoming king, right?"

"Yes," Caitlin said, "but it's a *story*!"

Mikey gasped. "Look! Merlin is disappearing!" They all turned to stare at the circling crows.

"It's amazing enough to go back in time," Rob whispered, aiming the camera. "But magic…?"

Mikey blinked, shaking his head. "Can someone really do things like that?"

Caitlin made a face. "It makes no sense at all. None of this does."

Rob nudged her. "Arthur's coming this way."

"I think Merlin expects us to help him," Bernardo whispered as they watched Arthur walk into the woods and head for the stream.

"I think we should," Rob said. "He looks like he's our age. He's got to be pretty scared." Rob clipped the digital camera back on his belt.

Arthur knelt to drink the cold water. Rob waited until he was finished, then he spoke quietly.

"Excuse me? Arthur?"

Arthur jumped to his feet. "Who are you?" His eyes widened. "Where do you come from?"

Rob explained, slowly and carefully, telling the story from the very beginning.

Arthur listened intently. "You must be magical then. Merlin is. I wish I could stay, but I must not tarry. The day will end soon."

Bernardo smiled. "We could go with you."

Arthur nodded. "I would welcome your company."

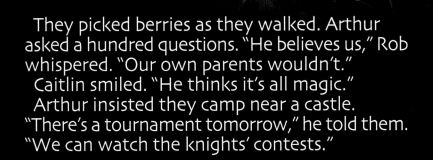

They picked berries as they walked. Arthur asked a hundred questions. "He believes us," Rob whispered. "Our own parents wouldn't."

Caitlin smiled. "He thinks it's all magic."

Arthur insisted they camp near a castle. "There's a tournament tomorrow," he told them. "We can watch the knights' contests."

Rob sighed. "We can't blend into the crowd."
"Maybe we can." Caitlin held up a pair of scissors.
She folded a camp blanket, cut a neck hole, then
an L-shape out of each side. "I brought needles
and thread. We'll stitch the sleeves and use the
scraps for hoods. I'll show you how."

The next morning was bright and sunny. Voices woke them up. The road to the castle was already jammed with travelers.

Arthur told them about his life as they put on the cloaks and hid their gear in the bushes. It was an amazing story. He had lived in a village until he'd met Merlin, the magician who had told him

DIGITAL ZOOM

F11/125 AUTO

he would one day be king. Since then, Merlin had been teaching him honesty, honor, and courage.

"And now he says I must pull a sword from a stone to claim my true destiny," Arthur said. "I wish I could just go back home."

No one spoke. They didn't know what to say.

Rob told Arthur they would meet him inside. As soon as Arthur disappeared into the crowd, Rob took out the digital camera and photographed the scene. Then he made sure all the gear was well-hidden and stepped out of the trees. The others followed, one at a time, joining the procession.

Mikey was nervous, but no one seemed to notice them. The people were laughing, shouting back and forth, pushing their way forward.

"Here we go," Bernardo said quietly as they neared the castle gates.

It took them a long time to spot Arthur; he was watching the knights' battle games. The Time Soldiers stared, fascinated as the jousts began. The knights balanced their heavy lances, galloping toward each other. The crowd cheered like people at a football game.

Bernardo squinted into the sunlight. The sword fighting was amazing, too. The knights' armor had to weigh 50 pounds or more, but the knights were agile, almost graceful, as they swung their heavy swords.

Mikey nudged Rob. "See that knight with the helmet that looks like some kind of a bird?"

Rob nodded. He tugged at Arthur's sleeve and pointed. "That knight is watching you."

Arthur sighed and nodded. "That's cruel Sir Edward. If I cannot pull the sword from the stone, he will become king."

Rob glanced at Caitlin. "Do the people know Arthur is supposed to become king?"

She nodded. "In most of the legends, yes, and some people tried to stop him. But no one knows if there even was a King Arthur or if he was just invented by ancient storytellers."

The Time Soldiers edged closer to the knights, watching the swordplay intently. One of the combatants managed to knock his opponent down and the crowd roared.

The herald blew his horn to announce the winner. "Skilled in tournament and in battle," he cried. "Sir Lancelot!"

The crowd got even louder.

Bernardo sighed. "I wish Jon could see this... and Adam and Mariah."

Rob heard a commotion and spun around. "Hey! Where are they taking Arthur?"

The others turned to look. Cautiously, they followed, weaving their way through the crowd.

Rob led the way, staying as close as he dared. The men went through heavy wooden doors of the castle and down a long, dark stairway.

Rob slowed down, motioning everyone to be silent. They hid, keeping in the shadows. The stone wall was cold and damp against Rob's skin, and the air smelled like moss.

It was hard to see at first. Then their eyes began to adjust. The Time Soldiers could hear Arthur's voice pleading, "I didn't do anything wrong!"

"Be still!" the guard ordered. His voice echoed off the stone as the sound of footsteps faded.

Rob went on, leading the way downward. There
was only silence for a time, but then they heard
footsteps again. The guards were coming back.
"We have to hide, fast!" Mikey whispered.
"There!" Brian pointed at an open door.

They slipped through it and found themselves in a huge room filled with armor and weapons. "The armorer repairs and makes weapons here," Caitlin said quietly. "That's the forge and... ." She stopped when the sound of the guards' voices came down the corridor.

Bernardo felt something run under his cloak. Startled, he kicked at it and saw a big rat scuttle out.

The footsteps in the hall stopped.

The Time Soldiers froze, exchanging glances, unsure of what to do.

"What was that?" one of the men asked. His voice was loud. It sounded like they were right outside the door.
"Be still!" Rob whispered to the others.

"It came from inside the armory," one of the guards said.

Mikey's hands were sweating. Caitlin held her breath.

"I know I heard something," the man insisted. Rob scratched lightly on the door.

"That?" his companion said. "That's just a rat."

"Maybe," the first man said. "But I thought I heard—"

Bernardo shooed the rat out into the hall.

"See?" the guard chuckled.

Caitlin exhaled, listening as the footsteps began again, then faded into silence.

"Let's go find Arthur," Rob whispered.

Arthur sat in a cell, scared and alone. He wished desperately that Merlin would somehow find out he was in trouble and come to help. He wished he'd gone straight to the village to find the sword in the stone as Merlin had told him to do. He was angry with himself.

Merlin would be angry with him too, and with good reason. He heard footsteps and sat up straight.

"Arthur? It's us. We'll get you out."

The whisper startled him and he scrambled to his feet.

"You have my gratitude," Arthur said as Rob
and Mikey strained to open the barred door.
Bernardo and Brian stood back to back, keeping
watch. Caitlin stood a ways off, listening for
footsteps. None came. Finally, the heavy plank
slid back and the door opened.

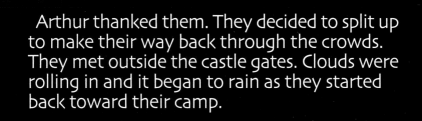

   Arthur thanked them. They decided to split up
to make their way back through the crowds.
They met outside the castle gates. Clouds were
rolling in and it began to rain as they started
back toward their camp.

"Should we go on with Arthur?" Rob asked the others as they hurried through the downpour. "What if the portal closes?"

Mikey shrugged. "It didn't in the dinosaur valley. Or when we rescued Julia. I think it waits for us."

"Does anyone want to turn back?" Rob asked.

They all shook their heads.

They hid in the trees until the rain slowed to a drizzle. When it stopped, they gathered their gear and started off.

Arthur smiled. "I am glad to have you as my companions."

They walked for hours. The Time Soldiers kept glancing back to see if anyone was following them. Then, on a hilltop, a thief sprang from behind the trees. "Give me your coins!" he demanded.

"Stand aside," Arthur commanded him.

The man laughed. "A boy who gives orders?"

"I am Arthur Pendragon, the one true king,

though I did not ask to be," Arthur said. Honesty shone in his eyes. The thief shifted uneasily — then bowed.

"I seek a sword trapped in stone," Arthur said.

The man pointed north. "There is a village a day's walk from here. Go straight until you cross the bridge, then follow the wide valley around to the far side of the mountain. You will find it there."

That afternoon, they crossed a creek. "Look!" Rob shouted. They all turned. The knight with the weird helmet was watching them. They ran into a forest so dense they had to stay in single file. Breathing hard, they stopped at the top of a rise. They could see a bridge spanning a wide,

deep gorge. But they had to cross a sloping meadow to get to it. They heard hoofbeats behind them. Sir Edward was making his way through the trees. Arthur and Rob looked at each other. They had no choice. Quickly, they all ran for the bridge.

Caitlin looked down at the river and hesitated. The hoofbeats were getting louder.

Rob tugged her sleeve. "Caitlin, come on!"

She nodded and forced herself to follow Arthur onto the bridge. The logs shivered and swung beneath their feet.

Mikey looked back to make sure Caitlin was all right. He smiled. No way Sir Edward could stop

them now. Then a flash of silver caught his eye.
It took a moment for him to understand: Sir
Edward was about to cut the bridge ropes with
his sword!

"Hang on!" Mikey shouted. An instant later,
the far end of the bridge dropped a few feet.

Rob stumbled. The camera he had clipped to
his belt came loose and fell into the chasm below.

The ropes snaked backward, dragged by the weight of the logs. Rob sprinted forward and jumped off the bridge. He helped the others onto solid ground—but Caitlin was too far behind. As the bridge collapsed, Bernardo managed to grab the rope. The others lined up behind him.

  Caitlin hung in midair. She could hear everyone calling to her, telling her to hang on. Their voices seemed distant, but she focused on them as she fought desperately to keep from falling.
  Inch by inch, the others pulled Caitlin upward. A few seconds later she was safely at the top.
  "That was close," Mikey said, trembling. "Too close."

The screens were still blank. "I wish they'd put their helmets back on," one of the men said. "Those helmet-cams worked perfectly."

"Maybe," said his companion, "we can get the mikes up if we push the bandwidth higher." He touched an icon on the screen and adjusted the levels.

"There, we have audio!" the first man breathed. They sat at the control board, listening.

"I have some good news," the first man said when the Time Soldiers fell silent for a moment. "Remember the quetzalcoatlus we lost when the T-Rex came through the portal?"

The man nodded. "You found it? Where?"

"A sandbar off Baja. Be glad it didn't head for a city."

"Everybody all right?" Rob asked.
Mikey and Bernardo were standing up, shaky
and breathing hard. Brian was bent over, trying
to catch his breath. Everyone nodded except
Caitlin.
"Caitlin?" Bernardo asked. "Are you hurt?"

"I'm OK," she said. Her voice was quivering, but she managed a smile. She took a deep breath and stared at the rough country ahead. The thief hadn't said anything about a tower.

"What will Sir Edward do now?" Rob asked
Arthur, staring at the angry knight on the other
side of the chasm.

"He will find a place to cross," Arthur said
sadly. "He thinks the kingdom should be his,
not mine. He won't give up."

Bernardo kicked a loose stone. "We can't

outrun a horse."

Rob was looking at the mountainside ahead of them. "We could go straight over the mountain, past that tower. It's too rocky up there for a horse."

Mikey nodded. "Then that's the way we should go, even if it's harder."

The mountainside was so steep in some places that they had to use their ropes to pull each other up. Their legs were aching when they finally made it to the top. Arthur looked back down the rocky slope. "We're safe here. No horse can get up those ledges."

Caitlin peered at the tower. "If it's abandoned, maybe we could spend the night here. We're

all pretty tired."

 "I'm not so sure," Mikey said. "Look at that green light."

 Rob signaled them to be quiet and they all listened for a long minute. There was only silence.

 Mikey stepped forward. "Let's go in and look around."

They walked quietly. As they entered a huge chamber, they could only stare in amazement. There were piles of jewels and other treasures— and a glowing green stone in a golden stand.

Rob exhaled. "Calico Jack had a stone like this, remember?"

Bernardo shook his head. "But those pirates were thousands of miles and hundreds of years from here."

Mikey turned around. "What's that smell? It's like scorched—"

Rob raised the flashlight. They all stepped back, stunned. "A *dragon*?"

Brian turned to run.

Arthur gripped his arm. "All of you, stay still and listen to me. Merlin has taught me about dragons. Fill your pockets with jewels. NOW!" His voice was so fierce they obeyed him without question.

The dragon rumbled and the stone walls shook. "Once we get outside," Arthur whispered, "throw the jewels in every direction, as far as you possibly can. It'll start searching, frantic to protect its hoard of treasure. With luck, it'll forget about us." He paused and took a deep breath. "Now run!"

As they ran out into the daylight, they threw the jewels as hard as they could. "Mikey, use your slingshot!" Rob shouted.

Mikey understood instantly. His slingshot would scatter the jewels three times as far. He aimed high to distract the angry dragon.

Arthur threw his handful of gems behind the dragon. "Hurry!" he shouted. "This way!" He guided them downhill and they ran, dodging plumes of dragonfire.

The scorched smell filled the air, bitter and sharp. The dragon kept rising, frantic, flying back and forth shrieking, searching for its scattered gems.

It forgot about the Time Soldiers completely.
They kept running. Hours later, they could still
hear the dragon's enraged roar.

Exhausted, they reached the bottom of the mountain and slept for a few hours. It was midmorning when they reached the village. People stared at them—they were not at all used to strangers.

"This place is amazing," Brian said, "like a movie set."

Arthur was trying not to get too nervous.
Caitlin showed him something called a compass
and tried to explain how it worked. He didn't
understand it, but he didn't ask questions. He
was worried. What if he couldn't pull the sword
out of the stone? If Merlin was right and he
somehow managed it, would he be a good king?

"There it is!" Rob said, spotting the sword stuck in the gray stone. Arthur stepped forward, staring. As he headed toward the sword, the villagers put down their tools and wares and followed.

As Arthur and the townspeople walked on, Rob glanced back. In the distance, he saw Sir Edward

riding toward them, whipping his horse into a pounding gallop. Rob motioned to the others to keep quiet. Arthur didn't need anything else to worry about right now.

"Did you see that? The dragon has the lost stone?" the man in the dark suit said. "If we could track them exactly, pinpoint the place and the time—"

"But we can't," his companion interrupted. "None of this makes sense in any case. Dragons don't exist and Arthur is a *legend*."

"There is some explanation," the first man said.
"Look! He's pulling the sword from solid rock!"
 The second man bit his lip. "Are you
suggesting—?"
 "What else can it be?" the first man demanded.
"Magic?"

"Go on!" one of the villagers urged Arthur. "If you are the true king, pull it free!"

They all began to shout.

Arthur looked up at the sky. He closed his eyes until the cheering and shouting died down. There were hoofbeats. Arthur ignored them. He focused

only on removing the sword from the stone.
 "Stop!" Sir Edward shouted, spurring his
exhausted horse closer, but it was too late.
 In a motion as graceful as sunrise, Arthur freed
the sword and raised it high. The Time Soldiers
cheered. The villagers shouted and danced.

Merlin was suddenly standing beside Arthur.
The Time Soldiers glanced at each other, astounded.
The villagers stepped back, gasping.
   "Behold the one true king," Merlin proclaimed.
"Tell your neighbors. Carry the news far and wide."
The villagers cheered and ran in every direction

to spread the news that the king of the legends
had arrived at last.

"You're too late," Rob shouted.

Sir Edward raised his fist in anger. He reined his
horse around and galloped away.

Merlin and Arthur walked all the way back to the portal with the Time Soldiers. They asked him questions about magic. He finally laughed aloud. "No more! You will find your own answers."

"How do you know?" Rob asked, but Merlin only smiled.

In the meadow, Arthur stared at the portal.

"You must go," Merlin told the Time Soldiers.

"You have little time."

"One more question," Rob pleaded. "The glowing green stone in the dragon's tower. What is it?"

Merlin's eyes narrowed. "You must find out for yourselves. Farewell."

"Thank you, my friends," Arthur said. "Farewell."

The Time Soldiers waved goodbye as they entered the swirling light.

When the Time Soldiers came out of the portal, Jon, Mariah, and Adam were waiting.

"One hour, exactly," Jon said. "We timed it to make sure. How long was it for you guys?"

"Almost three days," Mikey said. "We met King Arthur and Merlin and saw a dragon and—"

"Don't joke around!" Mariah pleaded. "We've been worried. Tell us everything that really happened and...." She studied Mikey's face, then glanced at Caitlin. "Really?"

Mikey nodded, and everyone started talking at once.

To be continued...

SCIENCE AND ARTS ACADEMY
1825 MINER STREET
DES PLAINES, IL 60016